Lyster Hoxie Dewey

The Russian Thistle

Vol. 15

Lyster Hoxie Dewey

The Russian Thistle
Vol. 15

ISBN/EAN: 9783337296841

Printed in Europe, USA, Canada, Australia, Japan

Cover: Foto ©ninafisch / pixelio.de

More available books at **www.hansebooks.com**

U. S. DEPARTMENT OF AGRICULTURE.

DIVISION OF BOTANY.

BULLETIN No. 15.

THE RUSSIAN THISTLE:

ITS HISTORY AS A WEED IN THE UNITED STATES, WITH AN ACCOUNT OF THE MEANS AVAILABLE FOR ITS ERADICATION.

BY

LYSTER HOXIE DEWEY.

PUBLISHED BY AUTHORITY OF THE SECRETARY OF AGRICULTURE.

WASHINGTON:
GOVERNMENT PRINTING OFFICE.
1894.

LETTER OF TRANSMITTAL.

U. S. DEPARTMENT OF AGRICULTURE,
DIVISION OF BOTANY,
Washington, D. C., May 5, 1894.

SIR: I have the honor to transmit herewith for publication a report on the Russian Thistle, by Mr. L. H. Dewey, assistant botanist. This report contains all the important information available at the present time on the subject, and is believed to indicate the best means of dealing with this weed. Whether or not the instructions here given are made effective rests on the industry and perseverance of the farmers who have to contend with it, nor can it be too deeply impressed upon them that the future grain product of some of our large wheat-raising areas depends largely upon their personal and united efforts during the next few years in restricting the growth of this plant.

Respectfully,

FREDERICK V. COVILLE,
Chief of the Division of Botany.

Hon. J. STERLING MORTON,
Secretary of Agriculture.

CONTENTS.

LIST OF ILLUSTRATIONS.

THE RUSSIAN THISTLE: ITS HISTORY AS A WEED IN THE UNITED STATES, WITH AN ACCOUNT OF THE MEANS AVAILABLE FOR ITS ERADICATION.

By LYSTER HOXIE DEWEY, *Assistant Botanist.*

A weed new to America made its appearance a few years ago in the wheat-raising region of the Northwest, and has already caused damage to the estimated amount of several millions of dollars. Spreading rapidly as it is over new territory and becoming more destructive in the region already infested, it threatens serious consequences unless prompt measures are taken to subdue it.

POPULAR AND TECHNICAL NAMES.

The plant is generally called Russian thistle in South Dakota and Russian cactus in North Dakota. Russian tumbleweed and other appropriate names have been suggested, but have not met the approval of popular usage. It is well known that the plant is neither a thistle nor a cactus, and that it is not even closely related to either of these groups of plants. The name Russian thistle, although not entirely satisfactory, is known and accepted by all who are familiar with the plant. The technical name by which it is known to scientists of all countries is *Salsola kali tragus.*

THE DEPARTMENT OF AGRICULTURE REQUESTED TO INVESTIGATE THE RUSSIAN THISTLE.

In October, 1880, a specimen of the Russian thistle was received at the U. S. Department of Agriculture from Yankton, S. Dak. It was supposed to be the common saltwort (*Salsola kali*) of the Atlantic coast, and the plant has been mentioned as such since that time in several botanical pulications, under the supposition that it was identical with the species of the coast region. No further complaints about the plant as a weed were received, however, until the fall of 1891, when specimens were sent in from Aberdeen, S. Dak., and Grand Rapids, N. Dak., with urgent requests for information which might aid in checking the spread of the weed. In the report of the Secretary of Agriculture for 1891 (pages 356 to 358), the plant was described, early fall plowing was

7

recommended as a check to its progress, and State legislation was suggested. In 1892 these complaints were received in increased number and from a wider area, although in most cases it was stated that, owing to the wet season, the weed was less troublesome than it had been during the dry season of 1891. A representative of the Department of Agriculture made a tour of investigation in the States of North and South Dakota, late in the year 1892, resulting in the publication of Farmers' Bulletin No. 10. The great demand for this report soon exhausted the edition. During the past dry season (1893) the weed reached an unusual development and the farmers became thoroughly alarmed at the situation. In response to requests from those most interested in exterminating the Russian thistle, a further investigation was made by the Department of Agriculture with a view to obtain information as to the extent of territory covered and the damage done, and especially as to the remedies which have been or may be applied to subdue or possibly exterminate the pest.

PLAN OF INVESTIGATION.

An assistant botanist of the Department of Agriculture visited the infested region, taking observations in the field and obtaining all possible information from those familiar with the plant. At the same time a circular letter was sent to the statistical agents of the Department, and a similar one to the register of deeds, in each county of North Dakota, South Dakota, Nebraska, Minnesota, and Wisconsin, the northern counties of Iowa. and the eastern counties of Wyoming.

This letter read as follows:

By reason of the urgent requests of farmers in the States of North and South Dakota, the U. S. Department of Agriculture has undertaken to ascertain the amount of damage which has been done in that region by the weed known as the Russian thistle, and to devise methods for concerted action to stop its progress and lessen the damage caused by it.

It is requested that you aid this investigation by answering the questions upon this sheet, returning the same in the accompanying franked envelope. A similar letter has been sent to each statistical agent in the area supposed to be infested by the Russian thistle. It is respectfully requested that this circular be returned within one week of the date of its receipt by you, even though you may not be able in that time to give answers to all the questions.

(1) Is the Russian thistle known in your county? ------------------------------

(2) What portion of the county is infested by it? ------------------------------

(3) When is it first known to have reached your county? ------------------------------

(4) In what manner was it introduced? ------------------------------

(5) How long has it been regarded as a really troublesome weed? ------------------------------

(6) What is your estimate of the amount of the damage done by this weed in your county during the past season? ------------------------------

(7) What is your estimate of the amount of damage done during each of the previous years in which it has been troublesome? --

(8) What proportion of the land in your county is under cultivation? --------------

(9) What are the principal crops grown in your county? ----------------------------

(10) What crops are especially liable to damage by the Russian thistle? ----------

(11) What factors are particularly active in spreading the weed over new areas?

(12) What methods have been used unsuccessfully in coping with the weed? ------

(13) What methods have been used successfully to reduce the damage caused by the weed? --

(14) Please inclose a twig of the Russian thistle, to enable us to positively identify the plant.

The present report is based on the investigations made in September and October, 1892, and November, 1893, together with the reports received in response to the circular letter, besides other correspondence and miscellaneous information.

POPULAR DESCRIPTION.

In May and June the seeds of the weed germinate, each sending up on a slender red stem two narrow green leaves about an inch long and somewhat similar in appearance to shoots of grass. Between these seed leaves a short stem soon appears bearing slender spine-tipped leaves which later produce branches in their axils (Plate III, Fig. b). These young shoots and leaves are tender and juicy, and are eagerly eaten by sheep, cattle, and horses. Until the dry weather begins the plants grow rather slowly, but they store up an abundance of moisture in the succulent leaves and branches. During the dry weather in August the moisture disappears from the slender leaves and they wither and sometimes fall off. New shoots are formed which at first are short and densely crowded with spine-pointed leaves less than half an inch long, but later elongate so that the leaves become separated at intervals of one-sixteenth to one-half inch (Plate III, Fig. a). Each leaf is accompanied by two bracts similar to the leaf itself, all spine tipped and projecting at almost right angles to the stem. A single, small, stemless flower grows in a cup-shaped depression formed by the bases of the two bracts. The outer parts, or perianth, of the flower are thin and paper-like in texture, spreading when fully open about one-fourth of an inch, and are usually bright rose-colored (Plate III, Fig. d). If the flower is taken out and carefully pulled to pieces a small, pulpy, green, coiled body appearing like a minute, green snail-shell will be found (Plate III, Fig. f). This is the embryo or miniature plant. As the seed ripens its coat becomes of a dull gray color, and at maturity the whole seed is about one-sixteenth of an inch in diameter, irregular in form, and of about one-half the weight of a flax or clover seed (Plate III, Fig. *e*).

During August and early September the plants become rigid throughout and increase rapidly in size, often growing 2 or 3 feet in height and 4 to 6 feet in diameter, forming a dense bushy mass of spiny branches (Plates I, II, and Plate III, Fig. *a*). By the middle of September the exposed parts of the plants have usually changed in color from dark green to crimson or rose-red. When the ground is frozen in November the entire plant, except the seed, dies.

The root, one-half inch or less in diameter, is broken at the surface of the ground by the force of the wind, and the plant is blown about as a tumbleweed, scattering seed wherever it goes. The seed remains inclosed in the paper-like perianth, and together with this is loosely held in its place by numerous twisted hairs, so that it is not readily shaken loose from the plant (Plate III, Fig. *c*). A plant may therefore roll about all winter and still retain some of its seed until the following spring. When the seed breaks loose from the plant the paper-like flower parts surrounding it act as a sail, so that it may be carried a long distance over the snow independently of the rolling plant. The seeds would not be carried through the air like thistle-down except in the case of very high winds and they would not be blown very far over bare ground.

A single plant of average size, 2 to 3 feet in diameter, and weighing 2 to 3 pounds at maturity when dry, is estimated to bear 20,000 to 30,000 seeds. Single plants have been found 6 feet in diameter, weighing about 20 pounds when thoroughly dry, and estimated to bear 200,000 seeds. At maturity the heaviest and strongest parts of the plants are the seed-bearing twigs. The inner branches receive little of the wear incident to tumbling about and are only strong enough to hold the plant together.*

---

* TECHNICAL DESCRIPTION.—*Salsola kali tragus* (L.) Moq. in DC. Prod., XIII, 2, 187 (1849).—A herbaceous, annual, diffusely branching from the base, 0.5 to 1 m. (1½ to 3 feet) high and twice as broad, smooth or slightly puberulent; tap root dull white, slightly twisted near the crown; leaves alternate, sessile; those of the young plant deciduous, succulent, linear or subterete, 3 to 6 cm. (1 to 2 inches) long, spine-pointed and with narrow, denticulate, membranaceous margins near the base; leaves of the mature plant persistent, each subtending two leaf-like bracts and a flower at intervals of 2 to 10 mm. (about one-twelfths to five-twelfths of an inch), rigid, narrowly ovate, often denticulate near the base, spine-pointed, usually striped with red like the branches, 6 to 10 mm. (three-twelfths to five-twelfths of an inch) long; bracts divergent, like the leaves of the mature plant in size and form; flowers solitary and sessile, perfect, apetalous, about 10 mm. (five-twelfths of an inch) in diameter; calyx membranaceous, persistent, inclosing the depressed fruit, usually rose-colored, gamosepalous, cleft nearly to the base into five unequal divisions about 4 mm. (one-sixth of an inch) long, the upper one broadest, bearing on each margin near the base a minute tuft of very slender coiled hairs, the two nearest the subtending leaf next in size, and the lateral ones narrow, each with a beak-like connivent apex, and bearing midway on the back a membranaceous, striate, erose-margined hori-

COMPARISON WITH SIMILAR PLANTS.

The Russian thistle resembles the two common tumbleweeds of the plains (*Amarantus albus* and *Cycloloma atriplicifolia*) more than any other species found in America. Like these its season of rolling is in the fall, and when blown into piles along the fences it is with difficulty distinguishable from them at a distance. The thistle differs from each of these species, however, in being spiny at maturity and in never bearing flat leaves. It is usually more densely branched than the former, and the branches are less slender than those of the latter, while the color of the dry rolling plant may be either dark or light, precisely like that of the second weed mentioned above. Both of these common tumbleweeds begin to roll about a month earlier than the Russian thistle.

ORIGIN AND HISTORY.

Nearly a century and a half ago this plant was mentioned by Linnæus as growing in eastern Europe, and many botanical writers have since described it among the plants of that region. The species *Salsola kali*, or some of its varieties, is found in most of the provinces of eastern Russia and western Siberia. The variety *tragus* seems to have developed on the plains of southeastern Russia, where the conditions are very similar to those of the Great Plains region of the United States. For many years it has been a destructive weed in the barley, wheat, and flax regions of southeastern Russia, and the cultivation of crops

---

zontal wing about 2 mm. (one-twelfth of an inch) long, the upper and two lower wings much broader than the lateral ones; stamens 5, about equaling the calyx lobes; pistil simple; styles 2, slender, about 1 mm. (one twenty-fifth of an inch) long; seed 1, obconical, depressed, nearly 2 mm. (one-sixteenth of an inch) in diameter, dull gray or green, exalbuminous, the thin seed-coat closely covering the spirally-coiled embryo; embryo, green, slender, about 12 mm. (one-half inch) long when uncoiled, with two linear subterete cotyledons. The plant flowers in July or August and the seeds mature in September and October. At maturity the action of the wind causes the root to break with a somewhat spiral fracture at the surface of the frozen ground and the plant is blown about as a tumbleweed. The mature flower with the inclosed seed is held in place in the axils of the bracts by the two minute tufts of coiled hairs, preventing the seeds from falling all at once when the plant begins to roll.

The variety *tragus* differs from the typical form of *Salsola kali*, which is common along the Atlantic coast, in the following characters: The leaves of the mature plant are very little longer than the leaf-like bracts which they subtend, while in the typical form of the species they are generally two to four times as long. The calyx is membranaceous and nearly always bright rose-colored, and the wings on the backs of the calyx lobes are much larger than the ascending lobes, while in the typical form the calyx is coriaceous and usually dull white or only slightly rose-colored, and the wings are thick, comparatively narrow, and less prominent than the ascending lobes. The species itself is less bushy in habit and less rigid at maturity. It has been known along the Atlantic coast from Massachusetts to Georgia for nearly a century and has never developed into a troublesome weed.

has been abandoned over large areas in some of the provinces near the Caspian Sea. No effectual methods of exterminating the weed are known in Russia. Sheep, pasturing on the young plants, aid materially in keeping the thistle in check, but it is continually growing more troublesome and extending to new territory.

The plant was first introduced into the United States in 1873 or 1874 in flaxseed brought from Russia and sown near Scotland, Bonhomme County, S. Dak. The land there is somewhat hilly, and corn is the chief crop raised, so that, owing to the wooded ravines and the standing cornstalks, the Russian thistle was at first slow in spreading. In 1877 it first appeared in Yankton County, east of Bonhomme, and five years later it had spread to the counties to the north and west of Bonhomme. It continued gradually to cover new territory until 1888, when it had infested most of the counties between the Missouri and James rivers south of the Huron, Pierre and Deadwood Division of the Chicago and Northwestern Railway. The strong winds during the winter of 1887–'88, followed by the dry summer of 1888, and possibly a fresh importation of seed into the flax fields of Faulk or McPherson counties, caused the weed to spread within two years to nearly all the remaining counties between the Missouri and James rivers in South Dakota and to infest the southern tier of counties in North Dakota. At about the same time it invaded northern Iowa and northeastern Nebraska. The dates on map 2 indicate approximately the years during which the Russian thistle first appeared in the counties thus marked.

PRESENT AREA COVERED.

Since 1888 the Russian thistle has been steadily spreading until now all of the counties of South Dakota east of the Missouri River and twenty counties in North Dakota are infested, and the plants have crossed to the west side of the Missouri River in at least four places in these States. Two counties in western Minnesota, three in northwestern Iowa, and four in northeastern Nebraska are thoroughly infested with the weed. Altogether this makes one almost continuous area of about 35,000 square miles which has become more or less covered with the Russian thistle in the comparatively brief period of twenty years. There are, besides, many isolated localities along the railroads as far east as Madison, Wis., west to Denver, Colo., and south to the southern border of Nebraska, in which plants have been introduced. The rapidity with which the Russian thistle has spread, both in infesting new territory and in thoroughly covering that already infested, far exceeds that of any weed known in America. Very few cultivated plants even, which are intentionally introduced and intentionally disseminated, have a record for rapidity of distribution equal to that of this weed. Throughout about 25,000 square miles it is very troublesome, and is causing a large amount of damage. Throughout the remaining 15,000 square miles, including most of the isolated localities, it is not yet so abundant as to cause much damage to crops, but it is established in sufficient quantity to scatter seeds and become troublesome during the next dry season.

MODES OF DISTRIBUTION.

PLANTS BLOWN BY THE WIND.

The most important mode of distribution of the Russian thistle, and the principal one furnished by nature, is the wind. In the winter when the ground is frozen, and especially when it is covered by dry, hard snow, the weeds are driven for miles by the strong wind, scattering seeds along their track, while gusts beat them about, covering with seed all the intermediate areas, and in blizzards, driving snowstorms, and sandstorms, the seeds themselves are carried to some extent independently of the plant. This natural means of distribution is unintentionally supplemented by other agencies supplied by man.

DISTRIBUTION IN SEEDS.

The Russian thistle was first introduced into this country in impure flaxseed, and this in the absence of good fanning mills continues to be the chief artificial agent of distribution. The seed is also carried in barley and oats, when these grains are not properly cleaned. It is said to have been found in wheat to some extent during the past year (1893). But unless the dry weather begins early the seed will not be ripe at harvest time, and if any mature plants should be threshed with the wheat the seed can easily be separated by even a moderately thorough use of the sieves and fanning mill of the thresher. Seeds are often carried in the threshing machines from one locality to another.

DISTRIBUTION BY RAILROADS.

Railroads form a third and highly important means of transportation for the seeds over long distances. There is every evidence that they are often carried to uninfested regions in the bedding or litter of stock-cars. These cars are sent to the stock-yards of Minneapolis, Chicago, Omaha, or Sioux City, but after unloading they are seldom cleaned at these places. They are sent, instead, with the litter and seeds to various shipping points, where they are cleaned if the amount of dirt or the nature of the cargo demands it. Rolling plants are sometimes blown into the trucks under the cars and into crevices in cordwood, machinery, etc., on flat cars, and are thus carried about the country.

TROUBLESOME CHARACTER.

The Russian thistle, although of some value as a forage plant when young, can be regarded only as a weed. It takes possession of valuable land as well as waste places to the exclusion of all other plants, and it draws from the soil a large amount of nourishment that might other-

wise go to useful plants. In these respects it partakes of the proper-
ties of all weeds, but it spreads and multiplies more rapidly, and hence
takes more space and more nourishment than most others, and unlike
them it seldom decays on the ground where it grows, to return to the soil
a portion of its substance.

DAMAGE TO CROPS.

In fields it is especially troublesome to wheat and flax. If a late
spring or rather early drought checks the growth of these crops, the
Russian thistle, growing at its best in dry weather, pushes up and
crowds or starves out many of the weakened plants, and the grade of
those which are left is much injured. In many flax fields and in some
wheat fields the crops in 1893 were left standing as not worth harvesting. The dry weather checked their growth, it is true, and aided the
growth of the weeds, but had it not been for the thistles, fair crops
might have been obtained. Barley and rye, though less important
products, are injured in about the same ratio as wheat. Oats, when
properly grown, often choke out the thistles, and hence escape injury.
If, on the other hand, they are sown thinly or on poorly prepared land,
the thistles may completely ruin the crop. Millet, the only grass
largely cultivated for hay in the Dakotas, is such a rank plant that it
is injured very little by any weed. Corn and potatoes are generally
thought to be injured but little by the Russian thistle, because these
plants are nearly mature before the thistles attain a large size, but it is
doubtful whether even these plants produce a maximum product when
badly infested. These crops, as well as beets, onions, and most garden
vegetables, may be kept free of the thistle by late cultivation.

INJURY TO MACHINERY, STOCK, AND FENCES.

Besides injuring crops the rigid bushy weeds make it very difficult
to run harvesting machinery. In many regions binders could not be
operated at all, and even the headers were used with extreme difficulty.
Plowing is often seriously interfered with by the large weeds, and every
farmer knows how troublesome it is to have the harrow or cultivator
continually clogging.

The sharp spines on the plants not only irritate and worry both horses
and men, but often, by breaking under the skin, cause festering sores
on the horses' legs, so that in many localities it has been found necessary to protect them with high boots or leggings. In handling grain
or flax, in the processes of hauling and threshing, the sharp spines cause
considerable irritation and consequent loss of time. On railroad grades
and other embankments these weeds choke out grass that would prevent the banks from washing.

During prairie fires the burning thistles cause a great amount of damage by crossing fire-breaks, which would otherwise be ample protection
to buildings or stacks, and by destroying wooden posts or fences. The

plant being compact and woody at maturity is better fitted to carry fire than any other tumbleweed in the prairie region The thistles bank up against wire fences, often completely covering them, and the force of the wind against the mass of branches often breaks the fence down, or if fire gets into them the posts are almost certain to be destroyed.

CONDITIONS FAVORABLE OR UNFAVORABLE TO GROWTH.

The Russian thistle grows best on high, dry soil, where it is not much crowded by other plants. It is seldom seen in sloughs or lowland, and makes no progress in the native prairie, except where the sod has been broken by badger burrows or by the overfeeding and consequent tramping of cattle on the ranges. In all places it is more abundant and more robust in dry seasons.

RELATION TO RAINFALL AND SOIL.

The thistles are less numerous and less robust in wet seasons, apparently not so much because they can not stand wet weather as because they are more crowded by other plants. Some Russian thistles at Ellendale, N. Dak., growing on the bank of an irrigating ditch, with their roots almost in the water, made a larger and more vigorous growth during the dry season of 1891 than any others in the dry soil about them. They grow on sand banks in the Missouri River, where the land is so often submerged that other weeds do not become established. At Minneapolis, in 1892, they grew well and spread rapidly in spite of 45 inches of rainfall before the end of the growing season.

The character of the soil seems to make comparatively little difference with the growth of the Russian thistle. Vigorous plants have been said to be an indication of poor soil, yet while this is certainly not true they may indicate poor farming. It is easier to kill them on good soil, since useful plants may be grown there to better advantage to choke them out. The thistle seems to grow almost equally well in all parts of the area occupied, except in light, sandy soil, such as the sandhills of western Nebraska. Here they are of slender growth and do not produce seed so abundantly as under more favorable conditions. This seed, however, when grown on good soil adjacent to the sandy region, produced apparently as vigorous and troublesome plants as any. The plants appear to grow equally well in alkaline soil or in soil that is not at all alkaline.

RELATION TO TEMPERATURE.

·The geographical range of the Russian thistle may ultimately be limited somewhat by the length of the season to which it is subjected. A severe frost will kill the plants at any time during their growing season and they usually require a period of three months after germination, from June until September, to produce mature seed. This time may perhaps be shortened somewhat by continued growth in higher latitudes, as most vegetation is quickened where the season is short. The plants produce seed abundantly in McHenry County, in the northern part of North Dakota, and are recorded as extending to northern Russia and to central Siberia. Doubtless it can adapt itself to climatic conditions so as to grow and produce seed as far north as wheat and flax can profitably be grown. It might be less troublesome in Manitoba because the frost would prevent some of the plants from maturing seed.

There are no data giving the effects of a warm climate on the Russian thistle in America, but plants will doubtless stand a temperature during their growing season as high as is found in most parts of the United States. The summer temperature during the day often exceeds 90° F. in the Dakotas. In southern Russia they are reported from the region of Tiflis and Baku, where the mean temperature is 50° and 60° F.

TOPOGRAPHY AND OTHER CONDITIONS FAVORING TUMBLEWEEDS.

The greater part of the region in which the Russian thistle abounds in this country is flat or slightly rolling plains land, with a general elevation of 1,500 to 2,000 feet above the sea. East of the Missouri River, in South Dakota, the general level is broken chiefly by the James, Vermillion, and Sioux rivers, all flowing south and emptying into the Missouri in the southeastern part of the State. These are all comparatively small streams, 2 to 4 rods wide, which flow through broad, shallow valleys. Even these apparently slight obstructions have offered for several years an effectual barrier to the natural passage of the thistle and, together with the north and south direction of the prevailing high winds, they account for the comparatively slow extension of the infested area to the east. There is no record that the plants have crossed the Missouri River at any place other than the ferries. These natural barriers to the progress of the weed are of only temporary benefit, however, as we have already seen that the seed is readily carried in many ways by artificial means. The plant spreads much less rapidly in a hilly region, such as the coteaus, or in the sandhills, or among the hills near the mouth of the Sioux River. They grow and thrive, however, in all these regions, and their comparatively slow progress even there is alarmingly rapid.

The absence of trees and fences over the greater part of the area infested favors the rapid distribution of the plants, and tree-planting and fence-building have been advocated as a means for restricting their progress. It would certainly be found ineffectual, however, for in some of the southern counties, where trees and fences are common and where there are hills, ravines, cornfields, and underbrush to obstruct the rolling plants, they are still making progress.

METHODS OF FARMING.

The methods of farming in the Northwest are particularly favorable to the distribution and growth of the Russian thistles. Wheat after wheat, with an occasional barren fallow but no cultivated or hoed crops, gives little opportunity to clear the land of troublesome plants. A few very profitable crops have induced farmers to break up more land than they can work well. Wheat is often merely drilled in on the furrow, or even in unplowed stubble land, and very seldom is given sufficient cultivation. The prairie soil will produce a fair crop under almost any conditions, and although it is generally conceded that a large yield on a few acres would be much more profitable than a small yield on many acres, little effort is made to attain this end. Where whole sections or even townships are one continuous wheat field or flax field, an acre here and there so grown to weeds as to be not worth the harvesting does not seem to have much bearing on the total amount, and the weeds are allowed to grow and ripen seed enough to cover a larger area the next year. They begin to grow large and coarse and to ripen seed soon after harvest; but at this time, when they most need attention, the farmer finds it difficult to get help enough even to secure his crops. The weeds are left, therefore, to take care of themselves.

Plowing in the spring or early summer for summer fallowing and then allowing the furrows to lie all summer without cultivation, a practice altogether too common, is especially favorable to the growth of the thistle. The seeds germinate and grow readily even if covered 4 inches below the surface. The thistles become well established in July and, being able to stand the dry weather better than other plants, they take complete possession of the land, and not growing thickly enough to crowd each other, they produce the large robust plants best fitted to roll. Nearly the same conditions exist in such potato fields as are little cultivated after the 1st of July. Prairie land broken up in the spring is liable to be covered with the Russian thistle in August, although none had grown on the land before it was plowed. The seed has been scattered in the prairie grass and germinates as soon as the sod is broken. Most of the large rolling plants grow on breakings, summer fallows, potato fields, fire breaks, along roadsides, and in tree claims, where the grass has been killed and where nothing has been planted thickly enough to occupy the land. They sometimes grow large in the flax fields if the flax is thin.

In grain fields, where the ground is shaded and the plants are crowded, the thistle is slender, bearing fewer and shorter branches. After the second year they are usually very abundant, so that with three weeks' growth after harvest they often completely hide the stubble. Plants growing in this condition will seed abundantly the field in which they stand, but they seldom acquire the form necessary for rolling.

WILL NOT THE RUSSIAN THISTLE DIE OUT NATURALLY?

This question has been repeated less frequently during the past season (1893) than during the preceding one. During the wet season of 1892, preceded by early frosts in the fall of 1891, the weed was less troublesome than during the previous year. The growth of the plant was temporarily checked, as it is likely to be by the same cause again; but the early frosts left enough seeds to propagate the weed in abundance, and the luxuriant growth of other plants, although crowding the thistles considerably, still left room for a great many to develop into robust tumbleweeds. Even the most favorable combination of seasons can have only comparatively slight effect in checking the growth or reducing the numbers of the Russian thistle.

In many instances it has been noticed that in small patches where the ground has become thoroughly seeded with the pest the plants come up too thickly to grow in their ordinary spreading habit, and, becoming slender and weak, are quite incapable of rolling. There is no record, however, of their becoming so thick over any large area that some plants did not find room to develop into very good tumbleweeds. What is true of small patches is only partially true of large areas.

In good prairie soil which has not been subdued by cultivation the Russian thistle, if left to itself, will finally be choked out by the native grasses. But there are many places, such as sandhills, bluffs, and dry lake beds, which would forever resist the encroachments of prairie grass. In Bonhomme County, where the Russian thistles have been growing for twenty years, they are as destructive now as they ever have been, and are as abundant and large as in any part of South Dakota. In Russia the plant has been known for one hundred and fifty years, and reports indicate that it is continually becoming more troublesome.

REMEDIES.

The plant is an annual, easily killed at any time during the growing season; it produces no seed before the middle of August or 1st of September, and the seed is short-lived. It therefore offers exceptionally favorable opportunities for being checked or even exterminated. For any effective measures, however, the two following principles must be rigidly adhered to:

1. No Russian thistle should be allowed to produce seed.
2. There must be concerted action throughout all the infested area.

If the Russian thistles, wherever found, should be killed before they produce seed, during three successive years, the pest would in all probability be completely exterminated. If the plants are destroyed over local areas, even throughout townships, counties, or entire States, and allowed to grow beyond the boundary lines, comparatively little advantage will be gained, for the rolling tumbleweeds will soon reseed the area cleared.

As a consequence of the lack of concerted action over large areas, no remedies have been found thoroughly effectual. Farmers who have tried to keep the weed from growing on their lands have so far succeeded in some instances that their crops have been little injured, but it has cost a great deal in extra labor, and they have been compelled to fight it every year because of seed blown in from adjacent areas. The farmer who has not attempted to drive the weed from his farm has sustained immense damage to his crops, and in some cases has been driven from the farm itself.

Wheat and other spring crops should be sowed as early as possible on well prepared land, so that the crop may get a vigorous start and shade the ground before the weeds germinate. The wheat may then be cut early, when there is less danger that the thistle plants will be large enough to cause trouble in the harvest field. If such a plan is followed, this and many other weeds growing in the stubble may be destroyed before they produce seed.

The land should be plowed as soon as possible after the wheat is cut, and if it can not be plowed before the 1st of September, the stubble should be burned. The thistle is still rather juicy in August and burns with difficulty, so that it is advisable to mow the stubble and let it dry a few days first. In this connection the importance of using a header in harvesting the grain is emphasized, as the greater amount of stubble left by this process furnishes material for a more thorough burning. The land should be plowed or the stubble burned immediately after harvesting a crop of barley, rye, or oats.

Crops like corn, potatoes, and beets should be cultivated thoroughly as late as possible. The extra cultivation will produce a better crop as well as kill the weeds. Several cornfields seen in the fall of 1893 evidently produced a much better crop of Russian thistles and pigeon grass than of corn, while other fields near these, in apparently the same kind of soil, but in which pigeon grass and the Russian thistle were entirely wanting, bore a corn crop 50 per cent better. Such crops should be cultivated until they thoroughly shade the ground, and, if the thistle appears after that, the hoe should be used so that none are allowed to produce seed. Potato fields and gardens devoted to early crops should receive better attention than heretofore. When cultivated only enough to produce a crop and allowed to remain with no cultivation after the middle of July, these places usually produce an enormous number of large thistle plants. Many such fields seen during the past and the preceding autumns might have been plowed for $5 or less, or even planted with a paying second crop, but instead were left to produce a crop of weeds, well fitted to cause hundreds of dollars damage.

If summer fallowing is practiced, the land should be plowed late in the spring, so that seeds near the surface may have germinated and the young plants be killed. The harrow or cultivator should be kept in use during the summer. The thorough cultivation will improve the condition of the soil for future crops as well as keep the weeds from seeding. This is the theory of summer fallowing, but, unfortunately, it has seldom been practiced in the Dakotas and adjoining States. The land there has usually been left untouched after the spring plowing. Instead of a barren fallow or "resting period," a crop of weeds is grown, which drains the land almost as much as a crop of grain, and the soil, instead of being cleared of weeds, becomes a veritable hotbed of them.

Summer fallowing, even if the land is kept barren by cultivation, gives comparatively little benefit except to clear out the weed seed. This object may be attained just as well by a cultivated crop which will pay the expenses of cultivation. A crop of beans, pease, clover, millet, or rye may be sown, pastured, and plowed under for green fertilizer at little expense, and it will improve the land vastly more than barren fallowing. Millet and oats combined may be grown and cut for hay. This crop will choke out nearly all weeds, while the few that do grow will be slender and weak, producing comparatively few seeds, and many will be cut with the hay before producing any seed. .

Sheep are very fond of the Russian thistle until it becomes coarse and woody. By pasturing sheep on the young plants they may be kept down, and the only known valuable quality of the weed utilized. In a few instances the half-grown plants have been cut and cured for hay, and one man even recommends raising the thistle for this purpose. Without careful analysis the nutritive ratio or comparative feeding value of this kind of hay can not be given, but it is doubtless much inferior to good prairie hay.

ROADSIDES, FIREBREAKS, AND WASTE LANDS.

If the Russian thistle is to be kept out of cultivated fields it must be exterminated along roadsides, firebreaks, waste land where the sod has been broken, and, in fact, in all places in which it has obtained an accidental foothold.

In many places the roads, which are usually mere unfenced driveways across the prairie, are lined on each side by hedges of robust Russian thistles growing between the beaten track and the prairie grass, as ragweeds grow along roads in the East. A road machine may here be used to good advantage, the scraper being set so as to take as thin a layer of earth as possible and throw weeds and all to the middle of the track. A single trip each way with the road machine would be sufficient in nearly all places to take the weeds on both sides of the track. If this work be done early in August, before the plants become large and stiff, the work of the road scraper may be sufficient, but if followed by a heavy roller the remedy will be made still more efficient and the road at the same time improved. When this work is neglected until the last of August or September the plants should be raked together and burned, though even with this treatment some seeds are likely to escape.

Firebreaks can be kept free from the Russian thistle and other weeds most economically by a frequent use of the harrow. When covered with large dry tumbleweeds, as they frequently are, instead of being a protection, they become a source of great danger in times of prairie fires.

In the sandhills, public lands, and the scattered weed patches on the cattle ranges there seems to be no direct compensation for the labor expended in exterminating the weeds. The thistles, however, must be exterminated in these places, and the work may be done at a cost small in comparison with the damage these plants would cause if allowed to produce seed.

The railroads have been important agents in distributing the Russian thistle, and in many instances it is positively known that the weeds which were allowed to grow along the railroad tracks subsequently spread to neighboring farms. During the past season (1893) the railroads in the thistle region have in general kept their right of way fairly clear of weeds. In traveling nearly 1,500 miles by rail in the thistle-infested region in November, 1893, the writer saw very few thistles growing along the railroad tracks, but thousands of plants were seen loose and blowing about on railroad land. In Nebraska, however, where the plant has not yet caused any trouble, it was frequently seen growing near the stations. The railroad weed laws should be enforced before the thistle becomes abundant and troublesome in new areas.

FENCES AND TREES TO KEEP THE RUSSIAN THISTLE FROM ROLLING.

All the remedies given above are directed toward destroying the plants before they have produced seed, and these are the only remedies, so far as known, which are effectual, or of which there should be any need, except care in cleaning seed. Too much thought and effort has been directed to catching or destroying the plants after they begin to roll. Tree-planting has been advocated, and if the methods of weed eradication employed in past years are to be used, trees may aid some-what. The timber claims throughout the greater part of South Dakota are so full of the Russian thistle that it is impossible to cultivate them, and they become a source of distribution instead of a barrier to it. A good growth of timber would certainly retard to some extent the rolling plants, but it would not be an effectual barrier.

It has been suggested that each farmer, whose land is not fenced, make a temporary fence by sowing about his farm each year a double row of sunflowers. The cost would be slight, and the fence thus made would doubtless aid materially in the fight, unless the sunflowers so abundantly introduced should themselves become troublesome weeds. The force of the wind against the weeds banked up against the sun-flower stalks would probably break them down during the winter; but when large banks had collected fire could be applied, and thousands of seed-bearing plants could be destroyed. The building of wire fences to stop the rolling plants is a remedy strongly advocated by some.

This scheme receives support from the fact that the few wire fences already erected become very prominent each fall for the great number of thistles banked against them. It is true that such fences catch thousands of weeds, but the fact is generally overlooked that an enormous number of seeds have already been dispersed before the plants are finally stopped.

IMPORTANCE OF CLEAN SEED.

One of the questions in the circular letters sent out for information reads, "In what manner was the Russian thistle introduced?" The two commonest answers to this question were "by the wind," and "in impure seed." The information received from these letters and from other sources indicate that carelessness in regard to the purity of seed sown is responsible for a large proportion of the damage done by the weed.

Grain and other seeds raised in the Dakotas are usually threshed by "thrashing crews," men who travel about with the machine and are hired by the owner or manager, so that all the employés about the threshing machine are more interested in the number of bushels coming out of the grain spout than they are in the purity of the grain. As a consequence, a great deal of material, such as weed seeds, broken stems, and other impurities that should go into straw stacks or chaff piles, finds its way into grain sacks and elevators. In many instances the seed threshed in this careless manner is stored and sowed the following spring without recleaning.

At the elevators and warehouses where farm seeds are commonly purchased two grades of seed are often kept for sale. The cheaper grade, dear at any price, is the uncleaned seed. From 2 to 20 per cent of the weight of the impure seed is cleaned out to make the better grade, and the difference in the prices of the two varies according to the amount of impurities removed and the cost of cleaning. The cheap grade is often purchased by poor or careless farmers in a vain attempt to economize, and the result is a crop of Russian thistles and other weeds instead of clean flax or grain.

A reasonable management of the sieves and fans in the threshing machines will separate Russian thistle seed from everything raised in the infested region except flax seed, clover seed, and millet, and these seeds may be cleaned by a careful use of the fanning mill.

Russian thistle seed usually has some of the papery flower-parts adhering to it even after passing through a threshing machine, and the size of the seeds with more or less of the parts adhering varies considerably, from naked seeds as large as those of clover to those with all the flower parts attached, increasing the bulk to the size of a melon seed. The individual seeds are a little more than one-third as heavy as those of flaxseed and about one-half as heavy as those of clover or millet, while an equal number in mass would be much more bulky than either.

If all the flower parts are cleaned off (and this rarely occurs), the naked seeds are very little larger than the seeds of red clover. Their rough coat and irregular form prevent them from passing through a sieve as readily as the smooth, rounded clover seeds, and, being much lighter, they can be easily blown out with the chaff by a careful adjustment of the fans. In the case of flaxseed the conditions are nearly the same. It would be more difficult to separate the seeds of Russian thistle from those of millet, as a grain of millet inclosed in the floral glume is slightly larger than the naked Russian thistle seed and only about one-third heavier. Many of the thistle grains in this case go into the screenings, but some doubtless go through with the millet. The thistle seeds with flower parts attached, as they usually are, would be very easily separated from almost any kind of seed, in fact it would be diffi- cult to adjust a fanning mill so that the light paper-like flowers would not be separated from the smooth grains of flax, clover, or millet, and none of the lighter grass seeds are used to a large extent in the Russian thistle region.

Although it is readily seen that Russian thistle seed may be easily cleaned from any of the seeds or grains raised in the infested region, it would certainly be safest not to purchase seeds for sowing which are known to have grown where these weeds are abundant, and under no condition whatever should the cheaper grade of seeds be sowed without recleaning.

LAWS REGARDING THE RUSSIAN THISTLE.

The only laws enacted to prevent the spread of the Russian thistle in particular are those which were passed by the legislative assem- blies of the States of North and South Dakota in 1890 and 1891, and are still in force on the statute books of those States. A copy of these laws is here given, for, if the provisions therein prescribed be carefully and faithfully carried out, the Russian thistle will soon be under com- plete subjection.

WEED LAWS OF SOUTH DAKOTA.

Duty of owners of land to destroy certain noxious weeds.

Be it enacted by the legislature of the State of South Dakota: SECTION 1. Every person and every corporation shall destroy on all lands which he or it may occupy, all weeds of the kind known as Russian thistle, Canada thistle, and cockle burr, at such time as the township board of supervisors, or the board of county commis- sioners, in counties which have not been organized into townships, may direct; and notice shall be published in one or more county papers for a time not less than three weeks before the time fixed upon for the destruction of said noxious weeds: *Pro- vided,* That if there be no newspaper published in the county, then the said notice, in lieu of such publication, shall be posted the same as election notices are posted.

Time fixed by township supervisors or county commissioners.

SEC. 2. It shall be the duty of the township supervisors or the board of county commissioners to fix the time for the destruction of all noxious weeds and to provide for their destruction in such manner as shall prevent their bearing seed.

Duty of overseers of highways.

SEC. 3. Every overseer of highways of every township or county shall also at the same time and in like manner destroy all such noxious weeds, either on the highways of his road district or on any unoccupied land therein, upon which the owner or lessee thereof shall neglect or refuse so to do, and for which service such overseer of highways shall receive as compensation a sum to be fixed by the board of county commissioners to be paid out of the general county fund: *Provided, however,* That the compensation for the said services shall not be less than two dollars per day.

Tax to be levied.

SEC. 4. It shall be the duty of the overseer of highways to present to the board of county commissioners an itemized account, verified under oath, showing description of each piece of land upon which noxious weeds have been destroyed in accordance with the provisions of this act and the amount of the charge for such service by separate items, and said amounts shall become a lien against the lands so described, except in case of the destruction of noxious weeds upon the public highways. The amount of cost of the destruction of such noxious weeds as so certified shall be placed upon the next tax list in a separate column, headed "For the destruction of noxious weeds," as a tax against the land upon which such noxious weeds were destroyed, subject to all the penalties thereof, and to be collected as other taxes, and the entry of such tax upon the tax list shall be conclusive evidence of the liability of the land to such tax.

Certificate to county clerk.

SEC. 5. It shall be the duty of all overseers of highways to certify to the county clerk in an itemized account verified by oath the amount of labor performed in destroying noxious weeds on all lands not public highways on or before the fifteenth day of September in each year.

Duty of county clerk.

. SEC. 6. It shall be the duty of the county clerk to enter upon the tax list, in a separate column for that purpose, headed "For the destruction of noxious weeds," an amount equal to the cost of such labor as a tax against all lands not public highways upon which such noxious weeds were destroyed.

Penalty for neglect to comply.

SEC. 7. If the owner or occupant of any such lands, or the board of county commissioners, or board of township supervisors in any county or township of this State, shall fail to comply with any of the requirements of this act, they shall forefeit to the county for such offenses a penalty of not less than five or more than fifty dollars; and upon complaint the State's attorney shall prosecute for any neglect of duty on the part of the owners or occupants of lands, overseers of public highways, board of county commissioners, or township supervisors. All forfeitures arising under the provisions of this act shall inure to the general fund of the county in which action is brought.

State's attorney—liability of.

SEC. 8. The State's attorney shall be liable under his bond for any failure to comply with the provisions of this act.

Repeal.

SEC. 9. All acts or parts of acts in conflict with the provisions of this act are hereby repealed.

Notice of landowners.

Sec. 10. Notice to the owners of the land provided to be given under the provisions of this act shall be made in the same manner as summons in the circuit court.

Emergency declared.

Sec. 11. Whereas an emergency exists, therefore this act shall take effect and be in force from and after the passage and approval.
Approved Mar. 7, 1890.
Session Laws, South Dakota (1890, pp. 271-273).

WEED LAWS OF NORTH DAKOTA.

Noxious weeds defined—manner of destroying to be prescribed.

Be it enacted by the legislative assembly of the State of North Dakota: Section 1. Every person and every corporation shall destroy upon all lands, which any such person or corporation shall own or occupy, all weeds of the kind known as Canada thistle, cockle burr, mustard, wild oats, French weeds *(Avena fatua*)*, and Russian cactus *(Salsola kali tragus*)*, at such time and in such manner as shall effectually prevent their bearing seed. Such time and manner of destroying such weeds shall be prescribed by the board of county commissioners, and the same shall be published at least two weeks in some newspaper in the county, not less than two weeks before the time so prescribed: *Provided further,* That if there be no newspaper published in the county, then written notices of the same shall be posted, the same as election notices are posted, in lieu of such publications.

Decision to be published.

Sec. 2. It shall be the duty of the board of county commissioners, at their regular meetings in April of each year, to determine the time and manner of destroying such noxious weeds and shall cause such decision to be published as provided for in section 1 of this act. They shall also cause to be mailed to the chairman of each board of township supervisors and to every overseer of highways and road supervisor in the county a copy of their proceedings.

When overseers shall destroy—tax against land.

Sec. 3. Whenever any individual, firm, or corporation owning or occupying any lands within this State shall neglect or refuse to comply with the provisions of this act for more than ten days after the time prescribed by said board of county commissioners, then it shall be the duty of the overseer or road supervisors, as the case may be, to proceed forthwith to destroy the same in the manner provided for said destruction by the board of county commissioners. It shall also be the duty of such overseers or road supervisors to destroy all such noxious weeds that may grow on the highways and school sections and timber-culture claims of his road district, and for so doing such overseer or road supervisor shall have such compensation, payable out of the township treasury or county treasury, as the township board of supervisors or board of county commissioners, upon presentation of his account thereof, verified by his oath and specifying by separate items the charges on each piece of land, describing the same, shall deem reasonable, and the respective accounts so paid, except for the destruction of such weeds upon the highways, shall be placed on the next tax roll of the township or county, as the case may be, in a separate column headed "For destruction of weeds," as a tax against the said land upon which such weeds were destroyed and be collected as other taxes, and the entry of such tax on the tax roll shall be conclusive evidence of the liability of the land so taxed to such tax.

---

* Corrected from the original.

Penalty.

SEC. 4. Whenever any overseer of highways or road supervisors shall neglect or refuse to comply with the provisions of this act, after having received notice as provided for in section 2 of this act, he shall be subject to a fine of fifty (50) dollars, and it is hereby made the duty of the State's attorney to enforce the provisions of this act.

Repeal.

SEC. 5. That an act entitled "An act to prevent the spread of noxious weeds in the Territory of Dakota," General Laws of 1885, Supplement and Chapter 102, Session Laws of 1890, relating to noxious weeds, be, and the same is hereby, repealed.

Emergency.

SEC. 6. Inasmuch as there is no provision for the destruction of noxious weeds, and many of said weeds will go to seed before July 1st, therefore this act shall take effect and be in force from and after its passage and approval.

Approved March 6, 1891.

Laws of North Dakota, 1891, pp. 253, 254.

It is evident from the preceding parts of this report that these laws are seldom complied with except in some cases by railroad corporations or by the more progressive farmers, who destroy the thistles, not because the law directs it, but because the best interests of their farms demand it. These laws seem to be enforced as well as are the weed laws of other States. The law in such cases can seldom be stronger than the sentiment of the community in which it is to be enforced. The chief hope, therefore, for subduing the Russian thistle lies not in legislating it out of existence, but in an earnest effort by each community and each individual, after seeing the advantage of destroying it and the danger of permitting it to grow, and after learning with what ease and certainty it can be eradicated, to carry out these measures. As the law may have some effect in the case of nonresident landowners and willfully ignorant or careless farmers, it should be enforced against them with all the healthy sentiment of the industrious farmers back of it.

PLATE I.

A Russian thistle plant of unusually compact form, densely branched, 3 feet high, 6 feet in diameter, and estimated to bear 200,000 seeds. This plant grew on rich cultivated land near Lamoure, N. Dak. The photograph was taken on the grounds of the Department of Agriculture, Washington, D. C.

28

PLATE I.

RUSSIAN THISTLE—COMPACT FORM.

PLATE II.

A Russian thistle plant of the ordinary form, loosely branched, about 1½ feet high and 3 feet in diameter. Plants of this form are common along roadsides and on uncultivated land where the turf has been broken. The specimen figured grew on a railroad embankment near Madison, Wis., and the Department is indebted to the agricultural experiment station of that State for the use of a photograph of it.

30

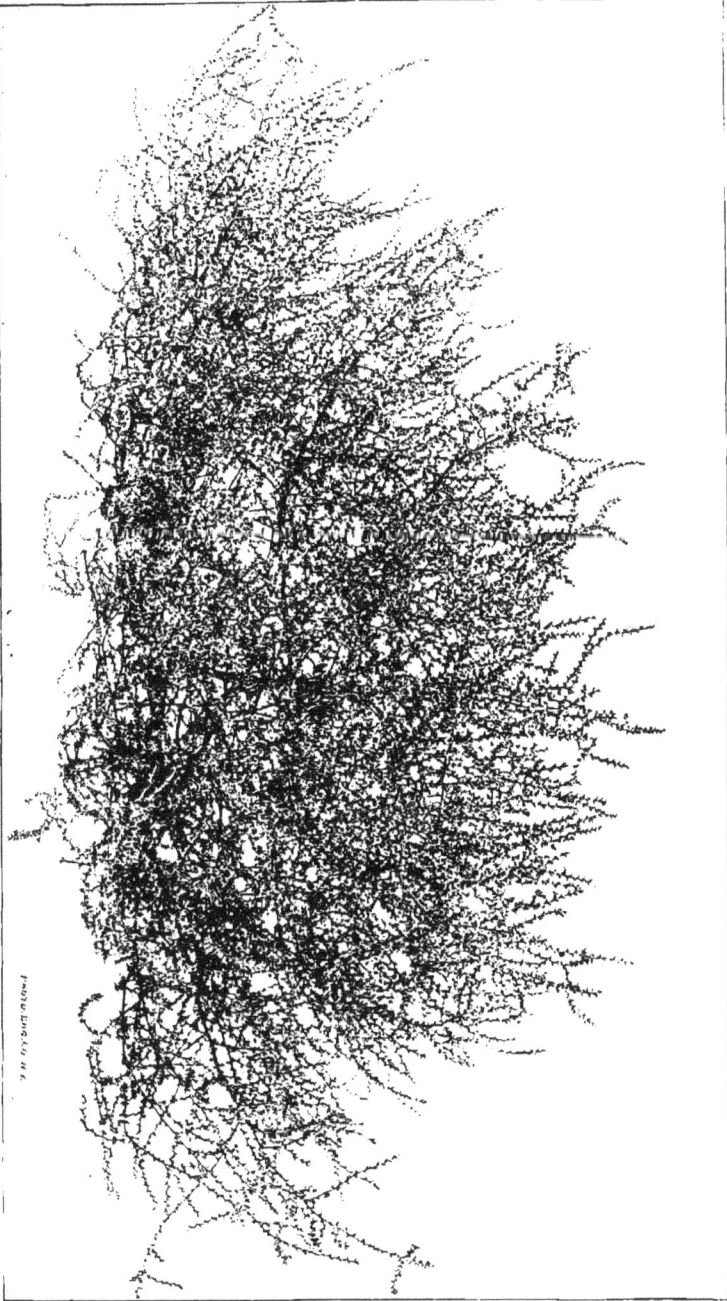

RUSSIAN THISTLE—ORDINARY FORM.

PLATE III.

Detailed figures of the Russian thistle: Fig. *a*. Branch of mature plant, natural size; *b*, seedling about two weeks after germination, natural size: *c*, flower detached from the axil and remaining suspended by minute hairs, in the ordinary inverted position on a rolling plant, enlarged 3 diameters; *d*, flower viewed from above and in front, showing the calyx lobes connivent into a cone-shaped body, and the large membranacous spreading wings, enlarged 3 diameters; *e*, seed with flower parts removed, enlarged 5 diameters; *f*, embryo removed from the seed, enlarged 7 diameters.

32

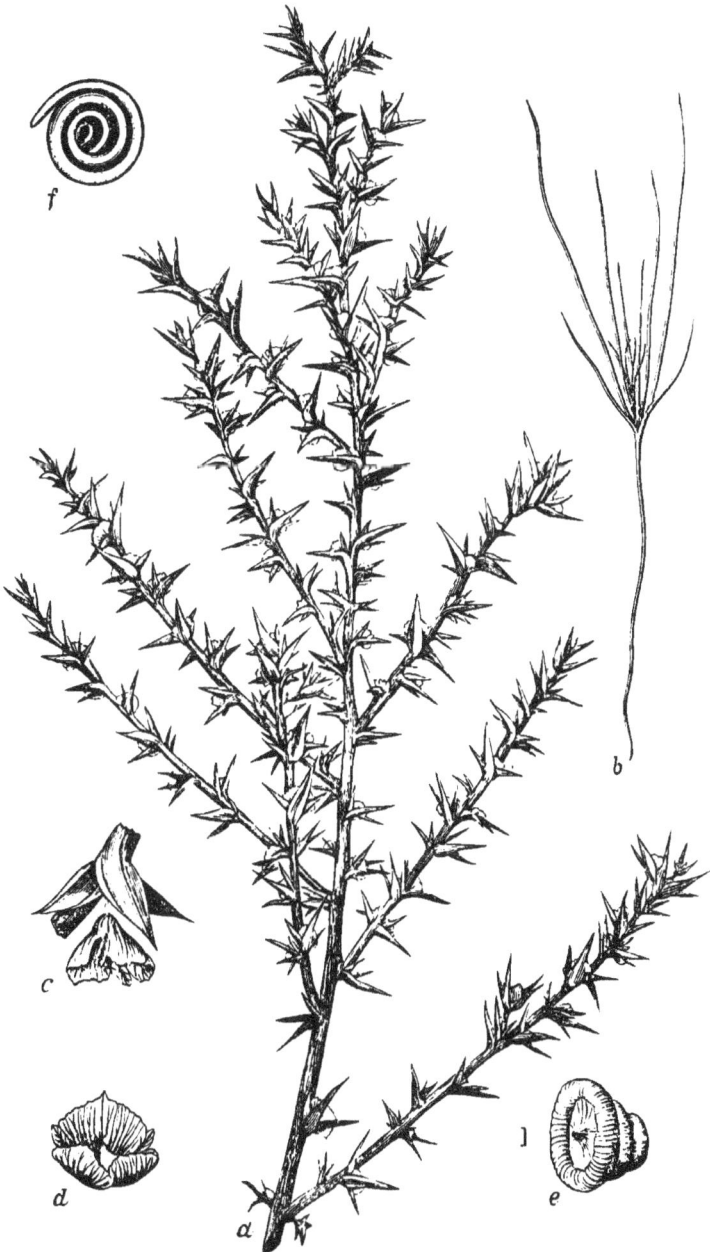

RUSSIAN THISTLE—DETAILED FIGURES.

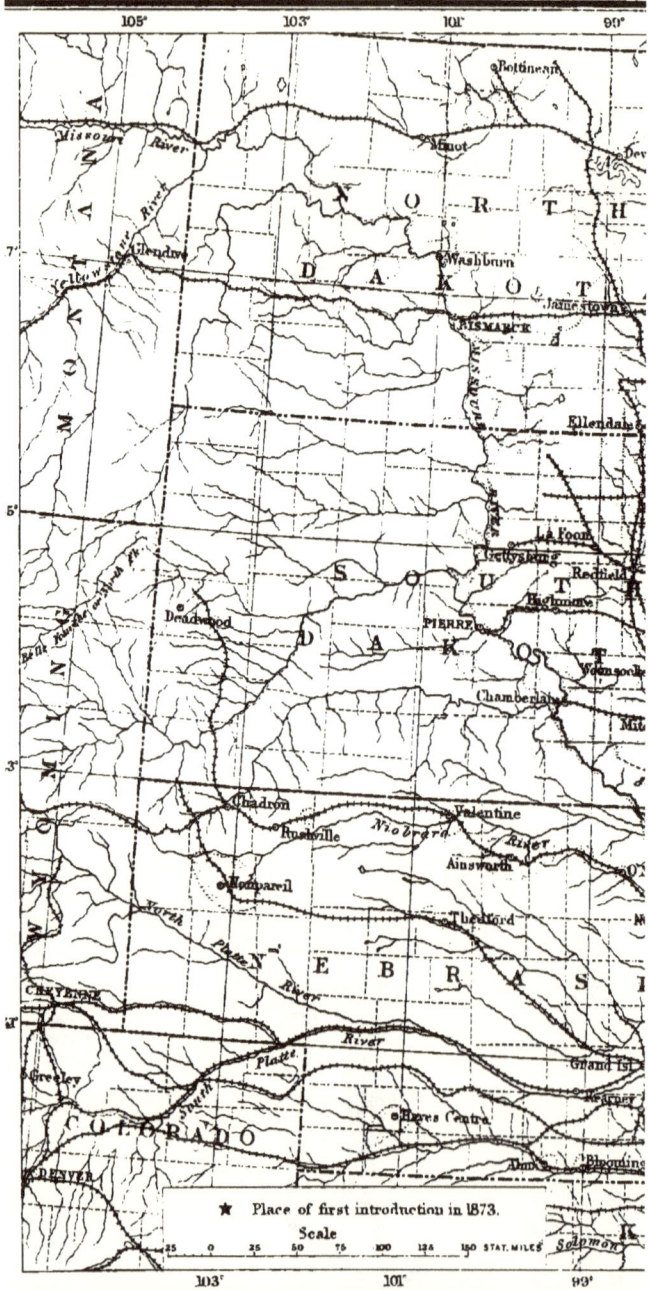

★   Place of first introduction in 1873.

Scale

25 0 25 50 75 100 125 150 STAT. MILES

DISTRIBUTION OF THE RU

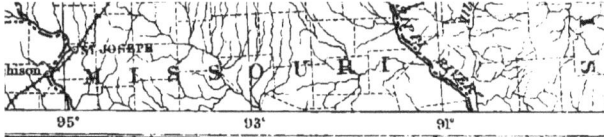

UNITED STATES IN 1893.

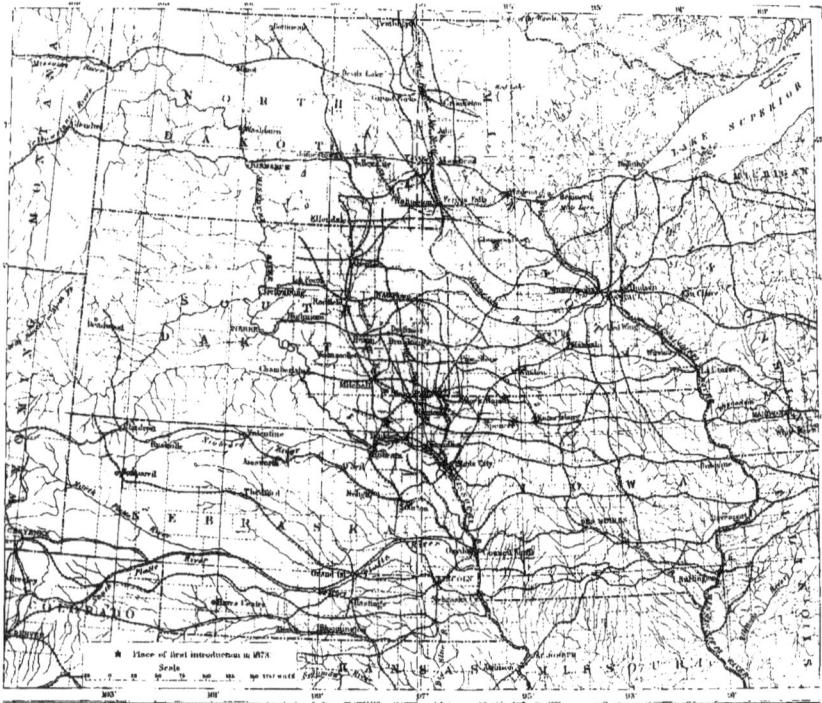

DISTRIBUTION OF THE RUSSIAN THISTLE IN THE UNITED STATES IN 1893.

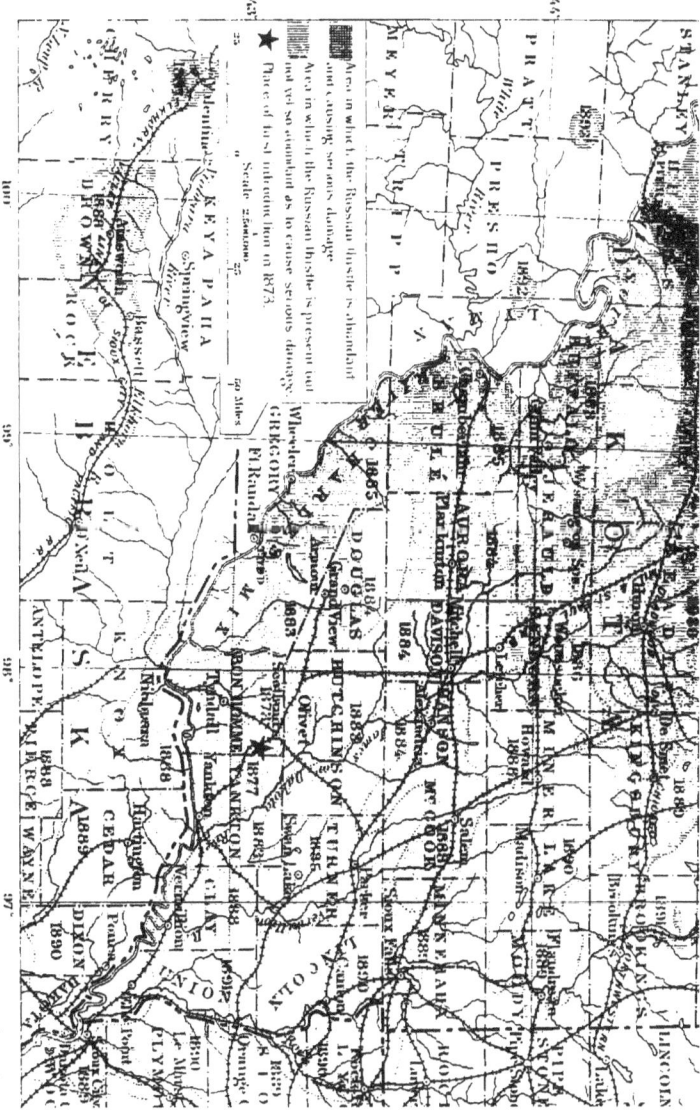

DETAILED DISTRIBUTION OF THE RUSSIAN THISTLE IN THE PRINCIPAL INFESTED AREA

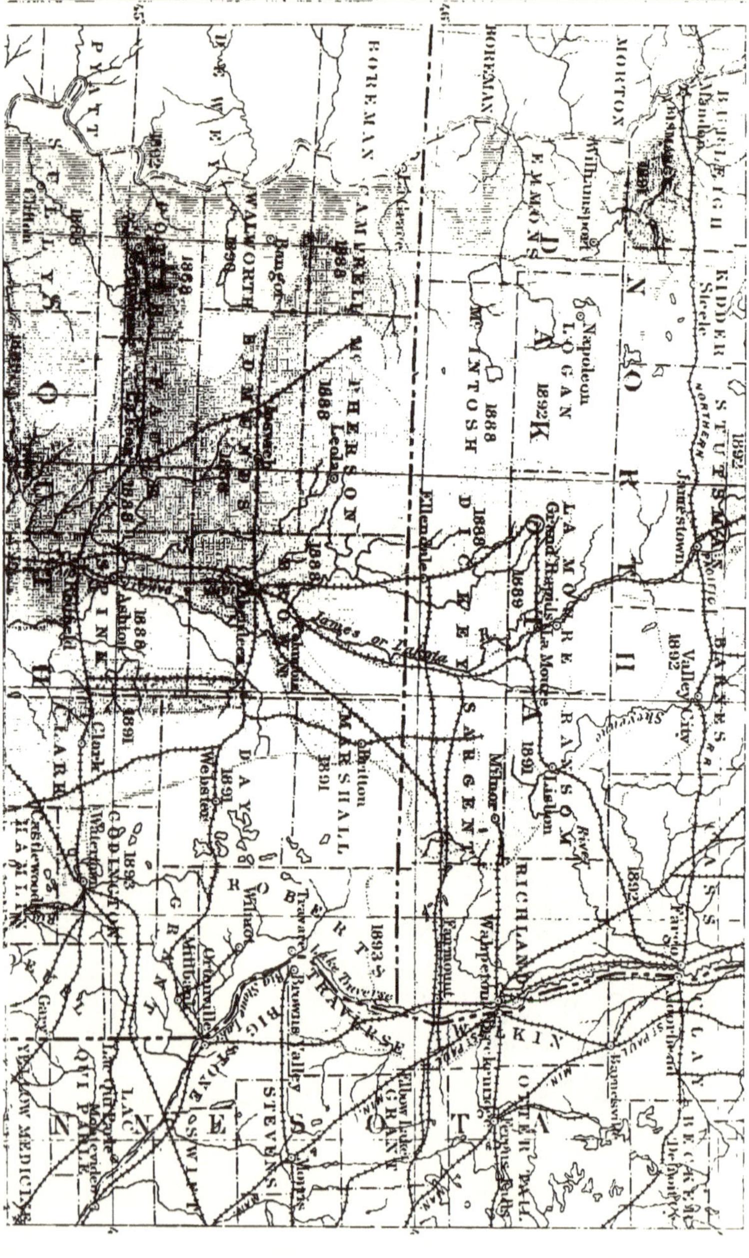
BURLEIGH
Mandan
Bismarck
KIDDER
Steele
STUTSMAN
Jamestown
BARNES
Valley City
CASS
Fargo
Moorhead
CLAY
BECKER
Detroit
MORTON
Williamsport
EMMONS
Napoleon
LOGAN
McINTOSH
LA MOURE
Grand Rapids
La Moure
RANSOM
Lisbon
Sheyenne
RICHLAND
Milnor
Wahpeton
Breckenridge
WILKIN
Barnesville
OTTER TAIL
Fergus Falls
DICKEY
Ellendale
SARGENT
CAMPBELL
WALWORTH
Bangor
McPHERSON
Leola
EDMUNDS
BROWN
Columbia
James or Dakota
MARSHALL
Britton
DAY
Webster
ROBERTS
Wilmot
Lake Traverse
TRAVERSE
Browns Valley
GRANT
Milbank
Ortonville
BIG STONE
STEVENS
Morris
SPINK
Ashton
CLARK
Clark
CODINGTON
Watertown
HAMLIN
LAC QUI PARLE
YELLOW MEDICINE
POTTER
FAULK
SULLY
NORTHERN PACIFIC

DETAILED DISTRIBUTION OF THE RUSSIAN THISTLE IN THE PRINCIPAL INFESTED AREA